To Gwénaëlle, who shares my passion for this job,
to our sons, Arzhel and Tenzor, and to our daughter, Daé.

my BEST

ALAIN DUCASSE

ALAIN DUCASSE
PUBLISHING

ALAIN DUCASSE

Which chefs taught you the most?

Before obtaining my diploma, I left the Talence Hotel School—things weren't moving fast enough for my liking. I then decided to knock on Michel Guérard's door. Already a star chef in the southwest of France, he took me on as his apprentice. Through him I met Gaston Lenôtre, with whom I learned the art of pâtisserie and desserts. Two years later, I joined Roger Vergé at the Moulin de Mougins, on the Côte d'Azur. He introduced me to authentic, natural, healthy Provençal cuisine. Alongside him, I learned the great advantages of simplicity in cuisine. But it was Alain Chapel in Mionnay, whom I joined in 1978, who influenced me the most. He was the first one to put the emphasis on quality produce, and at the same time, he revealed the truths of seasonality. No need to overcook. No need for frills. Rigor, flavor, and excellence were the key words in his highly contemporary cuisine, which marked me greatly.

How did you come to create the Louis XV in Monaco?

In 1986, as chef at La Terrasse in Juan-les-Pins, I had just earned two Michelin stars, when the Société des Bains de Mer asked me to manage all of the Hôtel de Paris restaurants. My special mission was the creation of a gastronomic restaurant, the Louis XV, and to obtain three stars in a maximum of four years! You can imagine the challenge. Franck Cerruti came on board with me for the dare, and we took the *cuisine bourgeoise* of the Mediterranean into the gilt setting of the palace. I wanted to prepare good home cooking and treat it in the manner usually reserved for ele-gant produce: dishes such as a vegetable casserole with bacon or roasted fruit, dishes cooked by our grandmothers and long forgotten by top notch restaurants, country fare that respected the seasons and, above all, used local produce. This was the type of cooking that appealed to me.

How do you manage to run more than twenty establishments in eight different countries from such a distance?

To explain how, let's back up to 1984: The airplane in which I was traveling crashed into the French Alps. For a year, I had no idea whether I'd ever walk again. What did I learn from that period of my life? I learned that it is possible to come to terms with oneself intellectually. At that time, the physical incapacity brought about by the accident forced me to imagine another way of cooking, and of long-distance management. I came to the conclusion that it is possible to run a kitchen without physically being there, but to do that, one must delegate and trust people—and, above all, train them. The transmission of knowledge is an essential value for me. I choose qualified, motivated partners, driven by the same passion and values as I am, to whom I convey my techniques and savoir faire. It is this guarantee of autonomy that enables us to produce great food. To ensure this training outside of my restaurants, I have created two schools, one for cuisine and the other for patisserie. I also have partnerships with schools abroad.

How would you define your culinary style?

My mental culinary map combines the cooking from my native southwestern France and the cuisine of the Mediterranean, which seduced me very early in my career. It is for this reason that the Bastide de Moustiers holds a very special place in my heart. I love simple but perfect food: one, two, or three flavors maximum. This is why we served a straightforward potato and bacon dish at the inauguration of the Alain Ducasse restaurant, on the Avenue Raymond Poincaré in Paris. The apparent simplicity of the dish does not preclude a great amount of work to attain perfection. On the other hand, I am also very curious. My roots provide support but never hinder or stop me from moving forward. I travel extensively, always in search of new discoveries. Wherever I go, what counts for me is genuine local product, because all

KEY DATES

September 13, 1956	*1990*	*2000*
Born in Castel-Sarrazin in the Landes region, southwestern France.	Obtains three Michelin stars at the Louis XV in Monaco.	Alain Ducasse opens at the Plaza Athénée.

good regional product, cultivated with love and respect on their own terroir, have unparalleled flavor. Without this, cooking is nothing. You must start at the beginning, the essential point where the tastes are real, and then permit them to express themselves with strength and subtlety.

How does your cooking evolve?

I have always advocated healthy, natural cooking, using sustainable ingredients, where fruits and vegetables take center stage. This is demonstrated in the all vegetable menus served at the Louis XV over the last twenty-five years. But what is relatively new is the awareness of the fragility of our planet's resources and the importance of respecting and treating them carefully. A chef must be responsive to the world around him, finding farmers, hunters, and fishermen who share these values and who respect ethics and biodiversity. Dietary habits are evolving. Dishes are lighter today and we eat differently from our grandparents, just as we shall eat differently twenty years from now.

What is your philosophy of life?

Always conquer obstacles and rise above my own limits to advance.

GOURMET
SNAPSHOT

1/ WHICH INGREDIENT AND UTENSIL CAN YOU NOT COOK WITHOUT?
Olive oil and a cookpot.

2/ WHAT IS YOUR FAVORITE DRINK?
Lillet, an aperitif wine from Bordeaux, and in particular, Lillet Blanc.

3/ WHICH COOKBOOK DO YOU ALWAYS HAVE AT HAND?
The *Grand Livre de Cuisine*, the first volume of my culinary encyclopedia, published in 2001.

4/ WHAT IS YOUR WEAKNESS?
Hot dogs in Manhattan.

5/ IF YOU HADN'T BECOME A CHEF, WHAT WOULD YOU HAVE LIKED TO BECOME?
An architect or traveler. Today, I am both of these and a chef!

6/ WHAT DO YOU COLLECT?
Travel trunks.

7/ WHAT IS YOUR MOTTO
More, faster, better.

2005
|
First chef to obtain three Michelin stars for each of his restaurants, in Paris, Monaco, and New York.

2011
|
Launch of Femmes en Avenir *("A Future for Women"), a training project for out-of-work women to help them find employment in the restaurant trade.*

CONTENTS

TABLE OF CON TENTS

RED MULLET,
NEW POTATOES, ZUCCHINI RIBBONS
AND BLOSSOMS, TAPENADE

48

ROASTED ROYAL
LANGOUSTINES,
CRISP MARINATED VEGETABLES

56

GRILLED PIGEON,
POTATOES WITH THYME BUTTER,
SALMIS SAUCE

64

MILK-FED
VEAL CHOPS,
TENDER YOUNG VEGETABLES
WITH SPRING GARLIC

72

RUM
BABA

80

WILD
STRAWBERRIES
IN WARM STRAWBERRY JUICE
WITH MASCARPONE SORBET

88

DUCK FOIE GRAS CONSERVED IN DUCK FAT

Cooking is about memories. My culinary path began in Chalosse, on the farm in southwestern France where I was born and grew up. Of these first years I particularly remember the aromas and flavors, intense memories that will always remain with me. When it came to deciding what we were going to eat, we would gather perfectly ripe vegetables in our kitchen garden. We had a strong, direct relationship with the cycles of nature. This foie gras is a tribute to my Landais roots.

RECEIPE

SERVES 6 - Preparation time: 20 minutes, 20 days in advance -
Cooking time: 30 minutes

DRINK PAIRING

A sweet white wine from the southwest, a Jurançon, for example. A red Graves from the Bordeaux region.

**DUCK FOIE GRAS
CONSERVED IN DUCK FAT**

- ❑ 2 ½ tsp (15 g) salt
- ❑ 1 tsp (3 g) ground white pepper
- ❑ ½ tsp (2 g) sugar

- ❑ 1 lobe raw foie gras, approx. 1 lb 5 oz (600 g)
- ❑ 2 ½ tbsp (40 ml) Cognac
- ❑ 8 cups or 2 qt (2 L) duck fat
- ❑ Fleur de sel (sea salt crystals)
- ❑ Coarsely ground pepper

GARNISH

- ❑ Country-style bread
- ❑ 12 small dried figs, halved

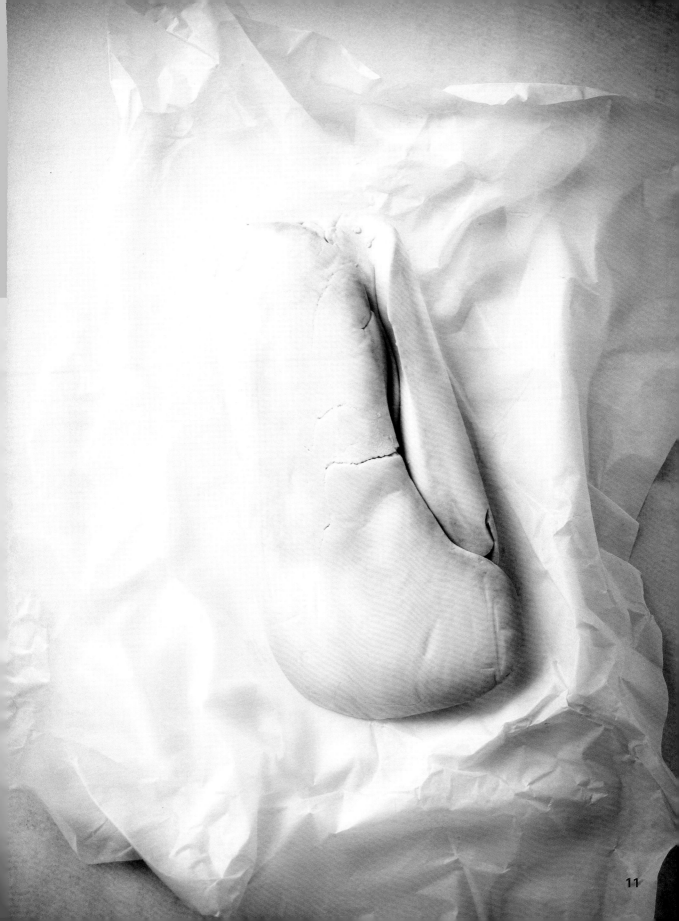

Combine the table salt, white pepper, and sugar. Season the foie gras evenly with this mixture.

Sprinkle with Cognac. Cover the dish containing the foie gras in plastic wrap and refrigerate overnight.

01

02

Remove the foie gras from the refrigerator 1 hour before cooking to bring it to room temperature. Heat the duck fat to 175°F (80°C). Immerse the foie gras with the domed side of the liver turned toward the bottom of the pan and cook for 15 minutes at 160°F (70°C).

03

Don't skimp on your choice of raw duck foie gras: It should be firm to the touch and without red spots.

Start cooking at 175°F (80°C). When the foie gras is added to the hot fat the temperature will decrease to 160°F (70°C).

Turn the foie gras and cook for another 15 minutes at 160°F (70°C). The heart of the foie gras should reach 105°F (40°C): Use a thermometer to verify the temperature.

Place the foie gras on a rack. Cover with plastic wrap and cool for about 2 hours. Set the duck fat aside* at room temperature.

In the absence of Cognac, you can use port, or Madeira wine, or Armagnac.

Place the cooled foie gras on plastic wrap. Wrap and tighten lightly to give the foie gras an attractive shape. Prick the plastic wrap with a needle to remove any air bubbles. Put the wrapped foie gras into a terrine.

06

Cover it with the cooled duck fat and store the terrine in the refrigerator for at least 20 days.

07

Duck fat can be purchased separately, ready for use. Above all, do not throw away the cold fat from the foie gras! It is perfect for sautéing potatoes, mushrooms, or steaks.

Unmold the foie gras. Place the terrine in a basin of hot water to the three-quarter mark, then slide a warm knife blade around the inside walls of the terrine to loosen the hardened fat. Carefully ease the cold fat away using the knife, being careful not to damage the foie gras.

08

Warm the knife blade in hot water and cut the foie gras into slices ¾-inch (1.5-cm) thick. Sprinkle with fleur de sel and coarsely ground black pepper. Serve with toasted country-style bread and fig halves.

09

With this method of preparation, you do not have to devein the foie gras. The 20 days of refrigerated conservation in the duck fat will "dissolve" the veins. Foie gras is best when served at 55°F (12°C).

GARDEN VEGETABLES
WITH BLACK TRUFFLE

Cooking demands respect for the ingredients. It took a certain amount of modest courage to serve this recipe at the Louis XV in 1987. Many found the dish too lowly; others found it almost provocative. To me, anything that brings out the wonders of the produce helps create beautiful cuisine; anything that distorts produce abases it. A chef must display humility before fine produce. With the focus on vegetables, this dish appeals to our current desire for health and fitness.

RECADE

SERVES 4 - Preparation time: 35 minutes - Cooking time: 30 minutes

DRINK PAIRING
*A white Châteauneuf-du-Pape from the southern Rhône Valley,
or a red Côtes de Provence wine.*

- ❏ 12 Cherry Belle radishes
- ❏ 8 carrots, with tops
- ❏ 8 baby fennel, with stalks
- ❏ 8 long white turnips, with tops
- ❏ 4 zucchini blossoms
- ❏ 7 oz (200 g) green beans

- ❏ 7 oz (200 g) garden peas
- ❏ 7 oz (200 g) baby fava beans
- ❏ 8 scallions
- ❏ 12 green asparagus spears
- ❏ 4 poivrade (purple) artichokes

- ❏ 1 pinch ascorbic acid
- ❏ 1 ½ tbsp (20 g) coarse salt
- ❏ ¾ cup (180 ml) extra virgin olive oil
- ❏ 4 cups (1 L) poultry fond blanc (see p. 97)
- ❏ 1 ½ oz (40 g) black truffle

- ❏ 3 ⅓ tbsp (5 cl) olive oil
- ❏ ⅓ cup (80 ml) truffle jus
- ❏ 1 ½ tsp (20 g) butter
- ❏ 3 ½ tbsp (50 ml) Barolo vinegar
- ❏ Fleur de sel (sea salt crystals)

Prepare the vegetables
Wash all the vegetables in cold water.
Prepare the radishes: Remove the small leaves and trim the stems evenly. Place in a bowl of iced water. Trim the carrot stems evenly, turn,* and place in the same bowl of iced water.

01

Remove the outer layer of the fennel bulbs, and trim the stalks evenly. Turn the turnips and trim the stems evenly. Place in a bowl of iced water. Remove the pistils from the zucchini blossoms, and fold the blossoms over. Refrigerate.

02

The cooking times for the vegetables will vary depending on the size. Check for doneness using the tip of a paring knife; the vegetables should be just tender.

Snap off the stalk end of the green beans but retain the tips. Cut into 1¼-inch (3-cm) pieces. Pod the garden peas and the baby fava, and sort according to size. Remove the root end of the scallions and trim the stalks evenly. Trim the asparagus spears, retaining only the tender tip. Cut off the large outer artichoke leaves and turn the artichokes, and then cut them in half. Set aside in a bowl of iced water containing a large pinch of ascorbic acid. Set the other vegetables aside in iced water.

Cook the green beans and scallions
Immerse the green beans and scallions in boiling salted water, when cooked, they should still be firm. Refresh* in iced water and refrigerate.

Cook the remaining vegetables separately. Proceed in the same way for each vegetable. Heat a little olive oil in a sauté pan* and gently pan fry* the vegetables without browning. Then, add some fond blanc to come to the halfway mark on the vegetables; cook covered.

05

Check for doneness using the tip of a paring knife. Turn the vegetables and their cooking juices out onto a baking sheet and chill rapidly.

06

Plunging vegetables into iced water stops them from cooking and sets their color.

Crush the black truffle with a fork. Use a sauté pan large enough to hold all the vegetables without crowding them. Add the cooking juices, a dash of olive oil from extra ripe olives, the truffle jus, and the crushed black truffle. Gently heat to warm the vegetables, add the garden peas and baby fava beans, and glaze* the vegetables in their juices. Add the green beans and scallions.

Arrange the glazed vegetables in soup plates.
Add the butter and Barolo vinegar to the vegetable cooking juices.
Adjust the seasoning if necessary and drizzle each serving with the jus.

At the last minute, if desired, you could grate a little truffle over each serving.

AUTUMN FRUIT AND VEGETABLE COOKPOT

Cooking is a permanent quest for discovery. This is something I try to adhere to, which began for me in childhood and continues to the present day via my profession. For years, I wanted to create a signature dish, a symbolic, almost philosophical expression of my cooking, which tells the tale of my origins. This could only ever be a vegetable dish, containing my favorite vegetables, the ones so present in my cooking for more than twenty years. They provide the thread connecting my own life with the many diverse sensorial experiences found in my restaurants. This cookpot is not only a cooking story; it also illustrates the harmony between form and content.

RECEIPE

Makes 1 large cookpot - Preparation time: 35 minutes - Cooking time: 45 minutes

Drink Pairing

*A dry white Loire wine, containing the chenin grape
variety; a Vouvray would be a good accompaniment.*

AUTUMN FRUIT AND VEGETABLE COOKPOT

- ❏ 1 large carrot (4 ¼ oz/ 120 g), with top
- ❏ 3 oz (80 g) yellow chioggia beets
- ❏ 3 oz (80 g) red chioggia beets
- ❏ 3 oz (80 g) celeriac

- ❏ 3 oz (80 g) pumpkin
- ❏ 3 oz (80 g) black radish
- ❏ 3 ⅓ tbsp (50 ml) extra virgin olive oil
- ❏ Fleur de sel (sea salt crystals)
- ❏ 6 ½ tbsp (100 ml) poultry fond blanc (see p. 97)
- ❏ Freshly ground black pepper

MATIGNON

- ❏ 5 ¼ oz (150 g) porcini mushrooms
- ❏ 1 white onion
- ❏ 1 ¾ oz (50 g) red apple
- ❏ 1 oz (30 g) Martin Sec pear
- ❏ 1 ¾ oz (50 g) fennel bulb
- ❏ 1 ¾ oz (50 g) cooked chestnuts

- ❏ 3 ½ tbsp (50 ml) extra virgin olive oil
- ❏ 4 tsp (20 g) butter
- ❏ 1 tsp (4 g) gray sea salt
- ❏ 1 ¼ tsp yellow curry powder
- ❏ ¾ tsp (3 g) fennel seeds
- ❏ Pepper

Prepare the vegetables

Wash all the vegetables. Peel the carrot and cut in two lengthwise. Peel the beets, celeriac, and pumpkin. Cut off the root of the radish and scrub the radish under warm running water. Cut all the vegetables into thin ⅒-inch (2 mm) slices using a mandoline, cover with a damp cloth, and set aside*.

01

Cut the sliced carrot, beets, celeriac, and pumpkin into discs using a sharp round cutter.
Cut the vegetable discs in half.
Cut the black radish slices in half. Cover the sliced vegetables with a damp cloth and set aside.

02

Use the vegetable trimmings to prepare a bouillon (see p. 99).

Prepare the fruit and vegetable matignon*
Cut off the soil-coated tips of the porcini mush-
room stems. Remove the caps and set aside.
Dice* the stems (brunoise*).

Peel and finely dice the white onion.
Wash and slice the apple, pear, and fennel bulb.
Crush the chestnuts with a fork.

Heat a large saucepan containing the olive oil over medium heat, then add the finely diced onion and
sweat*.
Add the brunoise and chestnuts and sear* to brown lightly. Add a little butter; season with salt and
pepper. Add the curry powder and pan fry* the ingredients for 2 to 3 minutes.

If porcini mushrooms are unavailable, you can use chanterelle or Portobello mushrooms.

Add the apple, pear, and porcini brunoise to the saucepan. Cook the matignon for about 10 minutes over low heat until fairly dry. Adjust the seasoning and stir in the fennel seeds. Transfer the matignon to a baking sheet and cool to room temperature.

06

Preheat the oven to 325°F (160°C). Spoon the matignon into the bottom of the cookpot, in an even layer. Then, cover with half-discs of vegetables, overlapping in alternating rows and leaving two-thirds of their surface exposed. Sprinkle with 4 teaspoons (2 cl) of olive oil, sea salt crystals, and freshly ground black pepper.

07

The fruit and vegetables used for the matignon are finely diced for even cooking.

Pour 3 ⅓ tbsp (5 cl) of fond blanc into the cookpot, cover, and place in the oven. Remove the lid after 15 minutes and finish cooking, uncovered for another 10 minutes. Remove the cookpot from the oven and let sit at room temperature for 10 minutes before serving.

Grate the porcini caps and sprinkle over the cookpot. Whisk the remaining fond blanc with 2 tablespoons (3 cl) of olive oil and the butter; serve separately.

The cookpot can be made in advance and served the following day; simply warm it briefly in the oven. The cookpot provides a full meal for one person or a vegetable accompaniment for two.

HAUTE-LOZÈRE PORCINI RISOTTO, BEEF JUS

Cooking is about unexpected encounters. During my training years I was fortunate to have many, including those with Michel Guérard, Roger Vergé, Gaston Lenôtre, and, above all, Alain Chapel. Later I met Paul Bocuse and other famous names, as well as unknowns throughout France and elsewhere. My chance meeting with Franck Cerutti, a passionate Mediterranean chef, was one of the most valuable. Franck had just returned from Florence, overflowing with the flavors of Italy, when he became my second in command at the Louis XV. The development of this risotto is largely his work.

RECIPE

SERVES 4 - Preparation time: 15 minutes - Cooking time: 1 hour 10 minutes

DRINK PAIRING

A red Bordeaux, such as a Pomerol.

PORCINI

- ❑ 12 porcini mushrooms, 1 ¾ oz (50 g) each
- ❑ 2 cups (500 ml) duck fat
- ❑ 1 sprig fresh thyme
- ❑ 5 cloves garlic, unpeeled and crushed
- ❑ 3 ½ tbsp (50 ml) extra virgin olive oil
- ❑ 1 ½ oz (40 g) dry-cured bacon
- ❑ ½ tbsp (20 g) butter
- ❑ Coarse salt
- ❑ Freshly ground pepper
- ❑ Fleur de sel (sea salt crystals)

PARMESAN LACE

- ❑ 3 ½ oz (100 g) Parmesan, grated
- ❑ 1 ½ tsp (10 g) all purpose flour

RISOTTO

- ❑ 6 ½ tbsp (100 ml) extra virgin olive oil
- ❑ 1 ¾ oz white onion, finely diced
- ❑ 7 oz (200 g) Arborio rice
- ❑ ¼ cup (60 ml) dry white wine
- ❑ 4 cups (1 L) poultry fond blanc (see p. 97)
- ❑ 2 ¼ oz (60 g) Parmesan, grated
- ❑ 2 tbsp (30 g) butter
- ❑ 6 ½ tbsp (100 ml) beef jus (see p. 96)

Prepare and cook the porcini

Cut off the soil-coated tips of the porcini mushroom stems. Brush the porcini with a little warm water, then wipe dry with a paper towel. Trim the mushroom stems. Finely dice the trimmings*and set aside for use with the rice.

Finely slice 4 mushrooms and set aside.

01

Melt the duck fat in a pan large enough to hold the remaining mushrooms in an upright position. Add the thyme and 2 cloves of garlic. Stand the 8 remaining porcini mushrooms in the pan, touching each other, so they remain upright during cooking.

02

Do not wash the porcini mushrooms in water as their sponge-like texture easily soaks up moisture.

Cook the porcini gently for 30 minutes over low heat. Set aside for 10 minutes, off the heat. Remove carefully from the duck fat and place on a rack to drain.

Prepare the Parmesan lace
While the porcini are cooking, combine the Parmesan and flour.
Sprinkle this mixture into a pan and heat gently until the ingredients blend, forming a white, lace-like crust.

Prepare the risotto

Heat a little olive oil in a pan. Add the finely diced onion, the porcini trimmings and sweat*. Add the rice and continue cooking for 2 minutes, until translucent. Deglaze* with the white wine and reduce until dry.

Pour the hot fond blanc over the rice and cook for 18 minutes on medium heat, regularly adding the remaining fond blanc. Finish by binding* the rice with the grated Parmesan and the butter, then add a little olive oil to give the rice a glossy sheen.

The fond blanc must be hot when poured onto the rice. If not, the cooking time will increase.

Cut the cooked porcini into thick slices. Heat a sauté pan* containing a little olive oil. Add the sliced mushrooms and the bacon and brown. Add a little butter and the remaining cloves of garlic. Cook until the garlic is golden; season with salt and freshly ground pepper.

Finish and presentation
Spoon the rice in small mounds onto flat plates. Do not press down on it.
Decorate with alternating slices of cooked and raw porcini. Spoon a little hot beef jus over each serving and top with a piece of Parmesan lace.

It is very important to stir the rice and fond blanc constantly while cooking: Stir three times in one direction and once in the other, then repeat. This movement helps the grains release their starch and the rice to cook evenly.

LOBSTER CASSEROLE
WITH TRUFFLE AND LUMACONI

Cooking requires freedom. I do not like dogma because it freezes tradition into a process of sterile repetition. I am even less fond of the confusion arising from chaotic combinations. Wonderful product is available everywhere and talent is the world's most evenly distributed asset. In this recipe, the Atlantic lobster and Mediterranean lumacomi pasta shells form a harmonious association. Freedom, in this case, was to arrange their meeting.

RECEPE

SERVES 4 - Preparation time: 40 minutes - Cooking time: 35 minutes

DRINK PAIRING

One of the exceptional Burgundies, such as a white Corton-Charlemagne grand cru.

- ❑ 15 black peppercorns
- ❑ 1 bunch fennel stalks
- ❑ ½ head garlic
- ❑ 2 ½ tsp (10 g) coarse salt
- ❑ 1 star anise
- ❑ 2 sprigs thyme
- ❑ 4 Brittany lobsters, 1 lb 2 oz (500 g) each
- ❑ 3 tbsp (45 ml) olive oil

- ❑ 3 tbsp (45 g) butter
- ❑ 4 cups (1 L) lobster fumet* (see p. 96)
- ❑ 3 ½ oz (100 g) black truffle
- ❑ 20 lumaconi pasta shells
- ❑ 20 confit* tomato petals
- ❑ Fleur de sel (sea salt crystals)
- ❑ Freshly ground black pepper

SEALING PASTRY

- ❑ 1 ¾ cups or 7 oz (200 g) cake/pastry flour
- ❑ ½ tsp (3 g) salt
- ❑ 2 ¾ oz (80 g) creamed butter*
- ❑ 1 egg
- ❑ 1 tsp white wine vinegar
- ❑ 1 egg yolk, beaten for glazing

LOBSTER BUTTER

- ❑ 10 tbsp or 5 ¼ oz (150 g) creamed butter
- ❑ Roe of 4 lobsters
- ❑ ⅓ bunch fresh basil

Prepare and cook the lobsters

Heat a large saucepan of water; add the peppercorns, fennel, garlic, coarse salt, star anise, and thyme. Simmer gently for 10 minutes.

Twist off the lobster claws at the joint near the head. Separate the heads from the tails. Insert a trussing needle into each tail to keep it straight while cooking.

Bring the water in the saucepan to a boil. Carefully slide the claws into the boiling water and cook for 2 minutes. Then add the tails and continue cooking for another 3 minutes. Refresh immediately in a bowl of iced water to stop the cooking.

In this recipe, the lobster heads are not cooked so that the roe remains raw.

Separate the claws at the first joint. Shell the claws, and "arm" them, removing the coagulated parts using a paring knife. Turn the tail over and use scissors to carefully remove the fine membrane. Cut the tails into even sections and set aside* at room temperature.

04

Heat a little olive oil in a pan, and sear* the pincers, elbows, and tail sections for 3 minutes. Add a teaspoon of butter at the end of the cooking.

Transfer the lobster pieces to a rack. Discard the cooking fat in the pan, then deglaze* with a little lobster fumet. Strain the lobster deglazing jus, and set it aside for later use.

05

06

Use female lobsters, as they have the most roe. You will be able to recognize a female because the first pair of swimmerets on the underside of the tail is soft and feathery.

Julienne* the truffle. Heat the remaining butter and a little olive oil in a pan; add the truffle and gently sauté for 2 to 3 minutes. Then, add the pasta and gently sauté over low heat. Moisten* with the remaining lobster fumet, cover and cook over low heat until al dente, then glaze*.

07

Finish and presentation
Reduce* the lobster deglazing juices by half. Add the confit tomato petals, and cook for several seconds. Bind* the sauce with a little butter. Season with salt and pepper, divide the pasta evenly between 4 casseroles with lids, then add the lobster.

08

Prepare the sealing pastry

Preheat the oven to 350°F (180°C). Combine the flour and salt, add the creamed butter, egg, and vinegar, and mix again. Roll out the dough to form a long ribbon ¹⁄₁₀ inch (2 mm) thick. Sprinkle lightly with a little water so that it will stick. Seal the casserole.
Brush the dough with beaten egg yolk and bake in the oven for 4 to 5 minutes.

Prepare the lobster butter

Mix the creamed butter with the lobster roe to obtain a smooth paste.
Set aside at room temperature.

Use a mortar and pestle to crush the basil leaves and bind* with the lobster butter. Serve the lobster in the casseroles.

This type of dough is used to hermetically seal the cover of a casserole, enabling its ingredients to cook in their own juices without losing flavor or evaporating.

RED MULLET,
NEW POTATOES, ZUCCHINI RIBBONS AND BLOSSOMS, TAPENADE

Cooking is a sensory pleasure. The five senses are unfailing guides for any chef and the best indicators of pleasure for gastronomes. Take a look at the pale pink of a red mullet fresh from the sea and admire its rainbow-colored dorsal fin—black, yellowy-orange, and white. And note how the purplish black of the tapenade highlights the bright green of the zucchini ribbons. When aromas waft up to our nostrils, our taste buds quiver in anticipation.

RECIPE

SERVES 4 - Preparation time: 35 minutes - Cooking time: 35 minutes

DRINK PAIRING
A red wine from Provence, such as a Bandol.

- ❐ 4 Mediterranean red
  mullets, 4 ¼ oz (120 g)
  each
- ❐ 2 sprigs marjoram
- ❐ Salt
- ❐ Freshly ground black
  pepper
- ❐ 3 ½ tbsp (50 ml) extra
  virgin olive oil
- ❐ 1 tbsp (15 g) butter

GARNISH

- ❐ 4 zucchini blossoms
- ❐ 2 zucchinis
- ❐ 7 oz (200 g) new potatoes
- ❐ 3 ½ tbsp (50 ml) extra
  virgin olive oil
- ❐ Fleur de sel (sea salt
  crystals)
- ❐ 1 tsp (5 g) butter
- ❐ 2 sage leaves
- ❐ ⅔ cup (150 ml) poultry
  fond blanc (see p. 97)
- ❐ Freshly ground black
  pepper

TEMPURA BATTER

- ❐ 6 ½ tbsp or 1 ¾ oz (50 g)
  all-purpose flour
- ❐ 6 ½ tbsp (100 ml) chilled
  water
- ❐ 4 cups (1 L) grapeseed oil
- ❐ Salt
- ❐ Freshly ground black
  pepper

TAPENADE

- ❐ 2 anchovy fillets, in brine
- ❐ 1 clove pink garlic, germ
  removed
- ❐ 9 oz (250 g) Taggiasca
  olives, pitted
- ❐ ⅔ cup (150 ml) extra virgin
  olive oil
- ❐ 4 tsp (20 ml) sherry vinegar
- ❐ Freshly ground black
  pepper

50

Prepare and cook the red mullets

Dress* the red mullets. Cut off each head with a knife. Make an incision in the belly of the fish, from tail to top. Lift the fillets: Slide the knife between both sides of the rib cage and each fillet, making sure not to detach them.

Using scissors, cut the backbone at the base of the tail and remove it with the rib cage. Scatter a few marjoram leaves over the fillets, reserving several for later user, and season with salt and pepper.

01

02

Heat a little olive oil in a pan. Brown each mullet on one side for 2 to 3 minutes, then carefully turn it. Add a little butter and a sprig of marjoram to the pan. Baste regularly during cooking. When cooked, place the fish on a rack.

03

You can make this recipe using red mullets filleted by your fishmonger.

Prepare the zucchini
Trim the zucchini blossoms at the base and cut in half lengthwise. Cover with a damp cloth and set aside*. Using a vegetable peeler, slice the zucchini into fine ribbons.

Prepare the potatoes
Wash the potatoes. Heat a little olive oil in a pan.
Slice the potatoes ¼-inch (1-cm) thick. Use the tip of a knife to round their angles. Sauté* the potatoes; when golden, season with salt. Turn the potatoes; add the butter and a sage leaf. Lower the heat, then add the fond blanc to come to the halfway mark on the potatoes. Cover, and when cooked, glaze*.

Flavor the olive oil with a sage leaf. Sauté the zucchini ribbons in the olive oil, add 2 tablespoons of fond blanc, cover, and when cooked, glaze*.

Prepare the tempura* batter
Combine the flour and the chilled water. Mix to a smooth batter. Put the bowl into a container of ice cubes.
Brush the inside of each blossom with tempura batter, then deep fry* in the grapeseed oil at 285°F (140°C) until crisp and golden. Drain on paper towels and season with salt and pepper.

To fry zucchini blossoms in a microwave oven, set out a sheet of plastic wrap, lay the blossoms on it, brush with olive oil, and cover with a sheet of plastic wrap. Cook for 1 to 2 minutes on maximum power, then dry.

Prepare the tapenade using a mortar and pestle

Soak the anchovies for 5 minutes in cold water to remove the salt. Put the anchovies and garlic into a mortar. Add the olives gradually, pounding with the pestle, to obtain a paste. Add the olive oil little by little, pounding constantly until thick. Add a dash of vinegar, a twist of freshly ground black pepper, and the reserved marjoram leaves.

08

Finish and presentation

Intertwine the zucchini ribbons and potato slices on each plate. Top with a red mullet, a little tapenade, and the zucchini blossom tempura to create volume. Serve the remaining tapenade separately.

09

ROASTED ROYAL
LANGOUSTINES,
Crisp Marinated Vegetables

Cooking is a long, ongoing apprenticeship. I was not born a Mediterranean; however, I've become one. My introduction to Provençal cuisine began with Roger Vergé at the Moulin de Mougins in 1977. Three years later I continued to learn and appreciate it at l'Amandier. Finally, I found myself at the Hotel Juana's restaurant, La Terrasse, in Juan-les-Pins. It was there that I first served these large roasted langoustines.

RECICE

Serves 4 - Preparation time: 35 minutes - Cooking time: 25 minutes

DRINK PAIRING
A white Burgundy such as a Saint-Aubin premier cru.
Or a blanc de noirs champagne.

- ☐ 4 royal langoustines
- ☐ 3 ½ tbsp (50 ml) extra virgin olive oil
- ☐ 1 tbsp (15 g) butter

VEGETABLES

- ☐ 4 vine-ripened tomatoes

- ☐ 7 oz (200 g) baby fava beans
- ☐ 3 ½ oz (100 g) extra-fine green beans
- ☐ 12 green asparagus spears
- ☐ 3 ½ oz (100 g) medium chanterelle mushrooms
- ☐ 4 poivrade (purple) artichokes

- ☐ 1 tsp ascorbic acid
- ☐ Fleur de sel (sea salt crystals)
- ☐ ¼ bunch chervil

VINAIGRETTE

- ☐ 3 ½ tbsp (50 ml) extra virgin olive oil

- ☐ 2 tbsp (30 ml) truffle juice
- ☐ Juice of 1 lemon
- ☐ Salt, freshly ground black pepper

CONFIT LEMON ZEST

- ☐ 2 Menton lemons
- ☐ 1 cube brown sugar

Prepare and cook the langoustines
Separate the langoustine heads from the tails.
Shell the tails, leaving the last two rings and the tail fan.
Even out the tail fans using scissors.
Insert a wooden skewer through the length of the each tail.

01

Heat the olive oil in a sauté pan*, and sear* only the back of the langoustine tails for 4 to 5 minutes.
Add a little butter at the end of cooking; baste the tails evenly.
Place the tails on a rack, underside up.
Cool at room temperature.

02

The langoustine heads and claws could be used to make a soup or bouillon.

Prepare the vegetables

Remove the stems, peel, and quarter the tomatoes. Seed* using the tip of a paring knife and dice evenly. Drain and set aside*. Pod the baby fava beans.

Snap off the green bean stalks; leave the tips. Cook in boiling salted water; refresh in a bowl of iced water, drain, and set aside.

Trim the asparagus spears.

Finely slice the asparagus, on the diagonal, leaving the tips whole.

Scrape the chanterelles. Wash in 4 to 5 changes of lukewarm water; set aside on a dry cloth.

Trim the artichokes, leaving 1-inch (2.5-cm) of stem, and cut in quarters. Set aside in a bowl of cold water containing a scant teaspoon of ascorbic acid to avoid oxidation.

Prepare the vinaigrette

Put all the ingredients in a bowl, whisk to combine, adjust the seasonings, and marinate for at least 10 minutes.

05

Prepare and cook the lemon zest confit

Using a vegetable peeler, zest the lemons and remove and discard the pith. Julienne* the ribbons of zest. Juice the lemons. Strain the juice into a saucepan and add the sugar cube.
Blanch* the zests ribbons, drain, and add them to sweetened lemon juice.
Cook until the mixture is dry, then set aside at room temperature.

06

Use untreated organic or Menton lemons to obtain the zest. If unavailable, use treated lemons but scrub well and wash before using.

Put all the raw vegetables into a salad bowl and season with the vinaigrette. Adjust the seasoning if necessary.

Preheat the oven to 350°F (180°C).
Finish cooking the langoustines on a rack in the oven for 3 to 4 minutes.
Place a serving of vegetables on each plate and top with a langoustine tail.
Decorate with sprigs of chervil and place julienned lemon confit on each tail.

GRILLED PIGEON,
POTATOES
WITH THYME BUTTER,
SALMIS SAUCE

Cooking is a *terroir*, a sense of place. It is also a marvelous way of gaining access to universal human truth by putting people in touch with nature. Cooking is like an intergenerational tapestry woven of threads linking the past and the present. It is another way of speaking our native language and living our culture. This pigeon breast recipe is one often made at the beginning of autumn, exposing an unknown side of Provence, that of the mountains... rugged...the land of Pagnol and Giono.

RECITE

SERVES 4 - Preparation time: 25 minutes - Cooking time: 55 minutes

DRINK PAIRING
A full-bodied red from the Languedoc.

PIGEONS

- ❑ 2 young pigeons, 1 lb 5 oz (600 g) each
- ❑ 4 thin slices lardo di Colonnata
- ❑ 4 sage leaves
- ❑ Salt
- ❑ Freshly ground white pepper

- ❑ 4 chilled medallions raw foie gras, 1 ¾ oz (50 g) each
- ❑ Fleur de sel (sea salt crystals)

POTATOES

- ❑ 12 new potatoes, 1 ¾ oz (50 g) each
- ❑ 4 cups (1 L) extra virgin olive oil

- ❑ ½ head garlic
- ❑ 1 sprig thyme
- ❑ ½ tsp (2 g) coarse salt
- ❑ Black peppercorns

SALMIS SAUCE

- ❑ 2 pigeon hearts and livers
- ❑ 2 sprigs flat-leaf parsley
- ❑ 2 sprigs chervil
- ❑ 3 chives
- ❑ ⅓ cup (80 ml) pigeon jus (see p. 97)

- ❑ 1 tbsp (15 ml) Sherry vinegar

THYME BUTTER

- ❑ ½ cup (120 ml) poultry fond blanc (see p. 97)
- ❑ 1 sprig thyme
- ❑ 5 tsp (25 g) butter, chilled

Prepare the pigeons

Singe and remove the feet and head; draw. Set aside* the hearts and livers. Remove the thighs.

Cut out the backbone using small scissors; remove the rib cage.

01

02

Lift the skin away from the breast and insert a slice of lardo and a sage leaf between the skin and the breast meat.
Pull the neck skin under towards the back.
Position the wings to hold the skin in place.

03

Use the pigeon carcasses and thighs to prepare the pigeon jus (see p. 97).
If necessary, you can always ask your butcher to dress, draw, and debone the birds for you.

Prepare the potatoes
Cook the potatoes in the olive oil with the garlic, thyme, coarse salt, and peppercorns.

Cut the potatoes into thick slices. Brush with oil and cook on a hot griddle. Give the sliced potatoes a 45 degree turn to create a crosshatch pattern.

Brush the pigeon breasts with garlic flavored oil. Season with salt and white pepper. Heat the griddle and grill the breasts for 15 minutes; turn occasionally. Do not overcook; the meat should be pink. Set aside on a rack. Place the chilled foie gras medallions on the griddle for several seconds.
Be careful, they cook very quickly.

When cooking the pigeon breasts, hold them in place with half a raw potato.

Prepare the salmis sauce

Finely chop the hearts and livers. Chop the herbs. Heat the pigeon jus in a sauté pan*, and bind* with the chopped hearts and livers. Add the herbs, remove from the heat, and infuse* for 10 minutes; add the vinegar.

07

Prepare the thyme butter

Pour the fond blanc into a saucepan and reduce* until the liquid is one-third of its original volume. Add the thyme and whisk in the butter.

08

The heart and liver are an integral part of a salmis sauce.

Debone the breasts using a deboning knife: Slide the blade down the length of the breastbone, as close to it as possible, to debone one side; repeat for the other side and the remaining breast.

Brush the potatoes with thyme butter. Mound the potatoes, foie gras, and pigeon breasts on plates. Drizzle with salmis sauce and sprinkle with fleur de sel and freshly ground pepper.

MILK-FED VEAL CHOPS,
TENDER YOUNG VEGETABLES WITH SPRING GARLIC

Cooking is generosity. Food has much more flavor when it is shared happily with others. The keys to really enjoying food are a beautiful, set table with friends around it and lively conversation. Here is a hearty but regal dish that one would be proud to serve to guests. I love these kinds of dishes because they embody the real reasons for a meal: friendship and conviviality.

RECIPE

SERVES 2 - Preparation time: 35 minutes - Cooking time: 1 hour 5 minutes

DRINK PAIRING

A red Burgundy, such as a Volnay. Or perhaps a red Chinon wine from the central Loire.

- ❏ 1 double rib of veal, 2 lbs 10 oz (1.2 kg)
- ❏ 3 ½ tbsp (50 ml) olive oil
- ❏ Salt
- ❏ 4 tsp (20 g) butter
- ❏ 2 cloves garlic, unpeeled and crushed

- ❏ 5 sage leaves
- ❏ 1 cup (250 ml) poultry fond blanc (see p. 97)
- ❏ ⅓ cup (80 ml) veal jus (see p. 97)

GARNISH

- ❏ 3 ½ oz (100 g) snow peas
- ❏ 8 carrots, with tops
- ❏ 12 scallions
- ❏ 12 new Noirmoutier grenaille potatoes
- ❏ Coarse salt
- ❏ 8 cloves spring garlic

- ❏ 3 ⅓ tbsp (5 cl) olive oil
- ❏ ½ tbsp (20 g) butter
- ❏ ½ cup flat-leaf parsley leaves
- ❏ 1 tbsp poultry fond blanc
- ❏ 3 oz (80 g) grated Parmesan

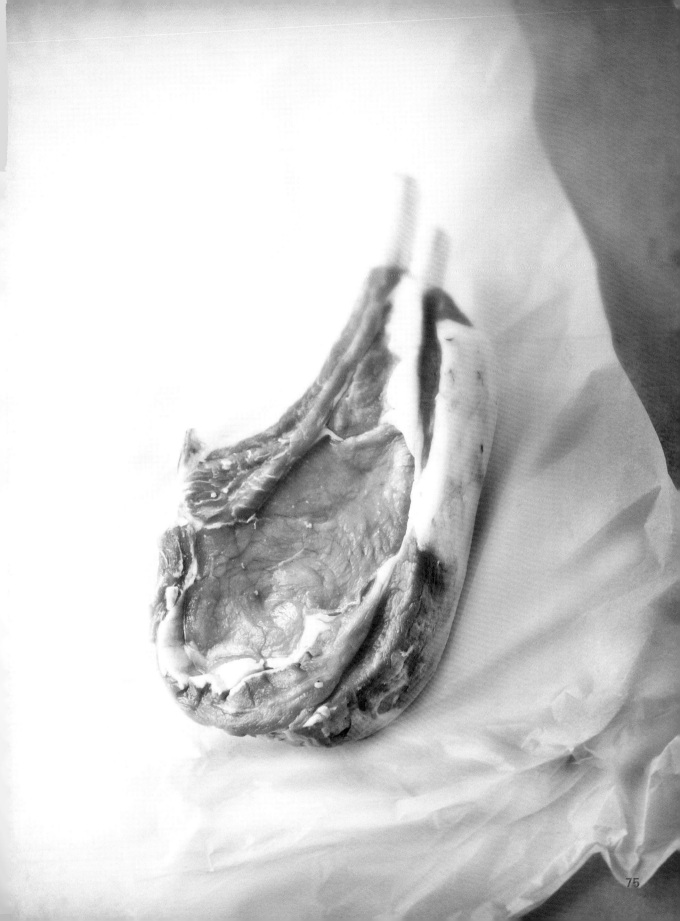

Ask your butcher to prepare the meat: Trim the double rib and remove the outer layer of fat. Expose 1½-inch (4-cm) of bone on the tips; truss the ribs. Cut the trimmings* and bones into small pieces.

Heat a little olive oil in a pan. Season the ribs with salt and brown each side and the fatty edge. Lower the heat and add a little butter, 1 clove of garlic, and 3 sage leaves.

01

02

Preheat the oven to 325°F (160°C). Finish cooking uncovered in the oven, basting regularly. Remove the ribs when the internal temperature reaches 135°F (56°C). Place on a rack, remove the trussing string, and rest for 15 minutes. Turn the cooked ribs every 5 minutes to allow the juices to circulate evenly inside the meat.

03

Use an appropriately sized pan for cooking meat. It will be more practical and ensure better cooking.

Prepare the jus

Discard all the fat in the pan used to cook the veal. Add a little olive oil and the veal trimmings and sear* until brown. Loosen the caramelized juices on the bottom of the pan using a spoon. Lower the heat and cover the trimmings using some of the cold fond blanc.

Bring to a boil and skim. Add the remaining sage leaves and garlic clove. Cook over low heat. Reduce* until syrupy. Add the remaining fond blanc and reduce by two-thirds. Add the veal jus and continue cooking until a syrupy consistency is obtained. Strain the mixture through a colander, then through a fine-mesh chinois*. Set the sauce aside* in a small saucepan.

Butter should be monitored closely when cooking. It heats quickly and burns at 250°F (120°C), making it difficult to handle.

Prepare the garnish

Remove the stalks from the snow peas, and cook in boiling salted water.

Wash and trim the carrot stems evenly. Turn*, cut into even pieces, and set aside. Wash and trim the root end of the scallions, then cut off and discard two-thirds of the green stems. Rub the potatoes with coarse salt to remove the dead skin, then rinse well, cut in half and set aside.

06

Heat a little olive oil in a pan. Sear* the carrots, then add the potatoes and sear. When the potatoes are brown, put a little butter into the pan and season with salt. Add the garlic and scallions and cook for a few minutes.

Add the parsley. Check the carrots for doneness with the tip of knife. They should be tender. Add the snow peas and deglaze* the pan with 1 tablespoon of fond blanc; glaze* the vegetables.

You can peel and slice the vegetables in advance. To prevent them from drying out, wrap in damp paper towels.

Finish and presentation

Place a pastry ring on eachplate and arrange the vegetables inside. Sprinkle with Parmesan and lightly brown the surface under a hot broiler.

Preheat the oven to 350°F (180°C) and reheat the veal for 5 minutes.
Reheat the jus over low heat.
Cut the veal in two lengthwise. Serve browned side up on top of the vegetables; glaze the meat with a little jus.

If you use a wooden chopping board, waterproof it with grapeseed oil from time to time.

RUM BABA

Cooking is about tradition, and this recipe is one of its symbols. For a gastronome, simply hearing the words "rum baba" makes the mouth water and conjures up an image of something delicious, moist and fragrant, syrupy and soft... in other words, a moment of perfect pleasure. To see a baba wearing its shiny apricot glaze, waiting to receive the anointing of aged rum, and ultimately to be accompanied by a vanilla cream is to witness a small masterwork of good taste. It is my favorite dessert, and you will find it on the menu at Monaco's Louis XV restaurant. This version was created in memory of the dessert served at the wedding of King Louis XV to Poland's Princess Marie Leszczyňska.

RECID

RECIPE

MAKES 10 BABAS · Preparation time: 35 minutes · Cooking time: 45 minutes

DRINK PAIRING
Feel free to replace the rum with Armagnac.

BABA DOUGH

- ☐ 1 cup + 4 tsp or 4 ⅔ oz (130 g) all-purpose flour
- ☐ ½ oz (6 g) fresh baker's yeast
- ☐ ¼ tsp (1 g) salt
- ☐ 1 ½ tsp (6 g) honey
- ☐ 3 tbsp (45 g) unsalted butter
- ☐ 3 large eggs
- ☐ 6 ½ tbsp (100 ml) grape seed oil

BABA SYRUP

- ☐ 4 cups (1 L) water
- ☐ 1 lb (450 g) sugar
- ☐ Zest of 1 lemon
- ☐ Zest of 1 orange
- ☐ 1 vanilla pod (seeds removed set aside)

APRICOT GLAZE

- ☐ 6 tbsp (75 g) superfine sugar
- ☐ 1 tsp (4 g) pectin NH
- ☐ ½ cup (125 ml) apricot pulp
- ☐ ½ cup (125 ml) baba syrup

VANILLA CREAM

- ☐ 1 cup (250 ml) whipping cream
- ☐ Seeds of 1 vanilla pod
- ☐ 2 tbsp (25 g) superfine sugar

Prepare the baba dough Combine the flour and yeast in a food processor bowl. Then add the salt, honey, butter, and 1 egg. Knead to obtain a smooth, glossy, elastic dough. When it pulls away from the sides of the bowl, gradually incorporate the remaining 2 eggs and finish kneading.

Place the dough on a lightly oiled baking sheet. Cover with plastic wrap and rest for 20 minutes.

01

02

Prepare the baba syrup
Put all the ingredients into a saucepan, bring to a boil, then cool.

03

Pectin NH is a natural gelling agent extracted from the skin and seeds of fruit. It is sold in drugstores and supermarkets.

Prepare the apricot glaze

Combine the sugar and pectin in a bowl. Heat the apricot pulp and the baba syrup in a pot to 105°F (40°C); add the sugar-pectin mixture. Boil for several minutes, then cool.

04

Preheat the oven to 350°F (180°C). Use 2-inch (5-cm) baba molds and brush with oil. Put 1-oz (30 g) of dough into each mold and tap the base on a work surface to expel any air bubbles. The dough will rise to the top of the molds and should be puffy.

Bake the babas until golden.

05

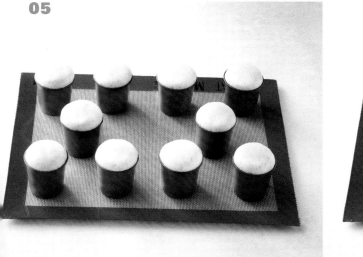

06

Cooking the babas takes 25 to 30 minutes. However, oven temperatures can differ, so color is the best guide.

Soak the babas in lukewarm syrup to avoid damaging. Set them aside to absorb the syrup and swell. Drain on a rack.

07

Brush the babas with the apricot glaze and set aside at room temperature.

08

Grapeseed oil is odorless and withstands high temperatures. It is ideal for frying (see p. 54) or for oiling molds.

Prepare the vanilla cream
Combine all the ingredients and whisk until light and frothy.

Place the babas in dessert dishes. Cut in half and drizzle the soft insides with rum.
Serve the vanilla cream on the side.

WILD STRAWBERRIES
IN WARM STRAWBERRY JUICE
WITH MASCARPONE SORBET

A kitchen needs a network of suppliers. What would chefs do without the tireless farmers and gardeners, mushroom gatherers, and fishermen returning with the daily catch? The supplier and the chef must have a perfectly interdependent and mutually beneficial relationship. I still remember the wild strawberries waiting for me in the morning when I arrived at the Louis XV. There they were, these tiny fruits from the woods, carefully placed on the table... precious gems nestled protectively in soil and leaves.

RECEIPE

SERVES 4 - Preparation time: 15 minutes - Cooking time: 1 hour 5 minutes

DRINK PAIRING
A Pineau des Charentes rosé.
Or a semisweet Bugey-Cerdon sparkling rosé wine.

STRAWBERRIES

- ❑ 1 lb 2 oz (500 g) wild
  strawberries

STRAWBERRY JUICE

- ❑ 6 tablespoons (70 g)
  superfine sugar

MASCARPONE SORBET

- ❑ 1 organic or untreated
  lemon
- ❑ 1 cup (200 g) superfine
  sugar

- ❑ 1 ½ cups (350 ml) water
- ❑ 4 ½ oz (125 g) fromage
  blanc (20% or 0% fat)
- ❑ mascarpone

Prepare the strawberries and juice

The day before, put the bowl of an ice cream maker into the freezer. Wash and hull the strawberries and place in a heatproof bowl. Sprinkle with the sugar and cover with plastic wrap. Refrigerate for 24 hours.

Place the bowl of strawberries in a bain-marie (water bath). Cook for 1 hour without removing the plastic wrap. Position a chinois over a bowl, and drain the strawberries for 15 minutes to obtain the juice. Do not press down on the fruit, as this is not a coulis.

01

02

Prepare the mascarpone sorbet

Zest and juice the lemon; strain the juice.

Combine the sugar and water; boil. When cool, add the lemon juice and zest.
Whisk the fromage blanc and mascarpone to combine.
Add to the syrup and whisk until smooth.

03

04

Before juicing a lemon, roll it on the work surface, pressing hard with the palm of your hand. This bursts the pulp cells, making it easier to juice.

Pour the sorbet preparation into an ice cream maker; process until firm but creamy.

Arrange the wild strawberries, tips up, in a dessert dish; pour over a little juice. Scrape the sorbet with a spoon to shape a quenelle. Warm the spoon in the palm of your hand and gently turn the quenelle onto the strawberries. Serve the remaining juice separately, pour the strawberry juice on the dessert just before serving.

To prevent a crust forming on the sorbet, place plastic wrap directly on the surface before storing it in the freezer.

GLOSSARY

GLOS SARY

BLANCH
Plunge an ingredient briefly into boiling water.

BIND
Thicken the consistency of a sauce or jus.

BOUILLON
A plain unfiltered broth or stock used for cooking and making sauces.

BRUNOISE
Fruit or vegetables cut into small, regular cubes for even cooking.

CHINOIS
A metal, cone-shaped strainer equipped with a very fine wire mesh. It is also known as a "Chinese hat" hence its name, which means "Chinese" in French.

CONFIT
Food, such as poultry, simmered and preserved in its cooking fat in a sealed container. The term can refer to other ingredients such as fruit saturated in sugar, garlic or tomatoes in oil, or lemons in vinegar (or brine).

COVER
Place a lid on a pan to assist the cooking process.

CREAMED BUTTER
Room temperature butter worked with a spatula until soft and smooth.

DEGLAZE
Pour liquid into a cooking pan to dissolve caramelized pan juices.

DICE
Cut into small cubes of even size.

DRESS
Prepare fish or poultry for cooking. For fish: trimming, scaling, gutting, washing. For poultry: singing, trimming, drawing, and trussing.

FOND BLANC
A clear pale sauce base: a bouillon or stock that has been clarified or filtered.

FRY
Cook food in oil or fat. Deep-fried foods are submerged in fat. Sautéed foods or pan-fried foods are cooked in just enough fat to coat the bottom of the pan and prevent food from sticking.

FUMET
A clear filtered stock obtained by simmering white fish bones and trimmings with water, vegetables, and herbs.

GLAZE
Coat food with the pan juices at the end of cooking. Or coat food with a thin, sweet, or savory liquid that will be smooth and glossy when set.

INFUSION
Aromatic ingredients soaked or steeped in hot liquid to obtain the flavor.

JULIENNE
Cut food into thin match-sticks. Commonly used for vegetables, citrus fruit zests, or bacon.

JUS
A jus can be made by reducing cooking liquid it to concentrate, and blend the flavors.

MATIGNON
Finely diced, simmered vegetables.

MOISTEN
Barely cover ingredients with stock or water at the start of cooking.

REDUCE
Boil a stock, cooking liquor, or sauce uncovered, to decrease the volume and concentrate flavors.

REFRESH
Plunge a hot, cooked ingredient immediately into iced water to stop the cooking process.

RISE
Dough, to which yeast has been added, will rise and expand in volume.

SAUTÉ
Cook food to a golden brown in a frying or sauté pan containing a little oil over high heat while turning or shaking the pan contents frequently.

SAUTÉ PAN
A round, flat-bottomed shallow pan with low sides, used for searing, sautéing, and pan-frying food.

SEAR
Start cooking food on high heat to quickly color and seal the surface.

SEED
Remove the seeds from a fruit.

SET ASIDE
Place ingredients or a preparation to one side for later use.

SWEAT
Cook an ingredient, without coloring it, in a small quantity of fat or oil over low heat to soften and eliminate part of its moisture.

TRIMMINGS
Parts of meat or vegetables unsuitable for presentation but that can be used to make and flavor certain preparations, such as stocks and sauces.

TEMPURA
A light, Japanese-style batter used to coat foods for frying.

TURN
Pare certain fruits and vegetables, cutting them into 7-sided barrel shapes.

BASIC RECIPES

BEEF JUS

Jus* base
- ☐ 4 ¼ lbs (2 kg) beef or veal trimmings
- ☐ 1 onion, 3 oz (80 g)
- ☐ 3 ½ tbsp (50 ml) extra virgin olive oil
- ☐ 6 ½ tbsp (100 g) butter
- ☐ 1 clove garlic, crushed
- ☐ 6 cups or 1 ½ qt (1.5 L) poultry fond blanc

Beef Jus
Makes ⅔-¾ cup (150-200 ml)
- ☐ 1⅛ lb (500 g) beef or veal trimmings
- ☐ 2 shallots
- ☐ 1 tbsp (15 g) extra virgin olive oil
- ☐ 3 ½ tbsp (50 g) butter
- ☐ 1 clove garlic, crushed
- ☐ 1 sprig thyme
- ☐ 2 ½ tsp (10 g) peppercorns
- ☐ 1 pinch salt
- ☐ ⅔ cup (150 ml) poultry fond blanc
- ☐ 4 cups or 1 qt (1 L) jus base
- ☐ Freshly ground black pepper

Jus base
Cut the trimmings into 1 ½-inch (4-cm) cubes. Peel and quarter the onion. Heat the olive oil in a saucepan; add the trimmings and bones and brown. Lower the heat. Add the butter, onion, and crushed garlic clove and brown lightly without burning. Discard the fat in the saucepan. Deglaze* and reduce, using a quarter of the fond blanc; repeat this procedure two more times. Moisten with the remainder of the fond blanc; cook gently for 3 hours. Strain the pan contents using a colander.

BEEF JUS (CON'T)

Then, strain the jus base using a fine-mesh chinois. When cool, refrigerate.

Beef jus
Cut the trimmings into 1 ½-inch (4-cm) cubes. Peel and slice the shallots ¼ inch (8 mm) thick. Heat the oil in a saucepan, add the trimmings and cook until golden. Add 3 ½ tbsp (50 g) of the butter, the shallots, crushed garlic clove, thyme, pepper, and pinch of salt. Cook gently for 10 to 15 minutes. Discard the fat in the saucepan. Deglaze and reduce using a third of the fond blanc; repeat this procedure two more times. Add the jus base and cook for 1 hour to 1 hour 15 minutes, until the jus is thick and coats the back of a spoon. Strain the jus and discard the pan contents. Then, strain again using a fine-mesh chinois. Add the remaining butter and season with pepper. When cool, refrigerate.

LOBSTER FUMET

Makes about 5 cups (1.2 L)
- ☐ 2 ¼ oz (60 g) fennel bulb
- ☐ 1 ¾ oz (50 g) white onion
- ☐ 1 clove garlic
- ☐ 7 oz (200 g) tomatoes
- ☐ 4 lobster heads
- ☐ 2 tbsp (30 ml) grapeseed oil
- ☐ 6 tbsp (80 g) butter
- ☐ 1 tbsp (15 g) tomato paste
- ☐ 2 tbsp (30 ml) Cognac
- ☐ ½ cup (120 ml) white wine
- ☐ 6 cups or 1 ½ qt (1.5 L) water
- ☐ Salt
- ☐ White peppercorns

Wash the vegetables. Finely chop the fennel and onion. Crush the garlic clove with the back of a knife blade. Quarter the tomatoes. Roughly chop the lobster heads. Heat the oil in a saucepan and sweat* the heads. Add the butter and caramelize. Add the fennel, onion, and garlic; sweat for 5 minutes. Add the tomatoes and tomato paste; cook for 3 minutes. Deglaze* with the Cognac and white wine. Reduce* to a thick shiny jus*, then add the water. Season with salt and a few peppercorns; cook for 30 minutes. Remove from the heat and strain the fumet using a chinois, pressing down on the lobster heads.

POULTRY FOND BLANC

Makes 2 qt (2 L)
Aromatic Garnish
- ❑ 1 white onion
- ❑ 2 carrots
- ❑ 1 small stalk celery
- ❑ 1 ¾ oz (50 g) Portobello mushrooms
- ❑ 3 stalks parsley
- ❑ 1 sprig thyme
- ❑ ½ bay leaf
- ❑ 4 white peppercorns
- ❑ 2 ¼ lbs (1 kg) poultry carcasses
- ❑ 10 cups or 2 ½ qt (2.5 L) water
- ❑ 1 chicken bouillon cube
- ❑ 1 tsp (5 g) coarse salt

Wash, peel, and finely chop all the vegetables and aromatic garnish. Wrap the peppercorns in muslin and secure with string. Trim the carcasses of all fat and blood and wash under running water. Place in a large saucepan, cover with cold water and bring to a boil over high heat. As soon as the water boils, remove from the heat, discard the water, drain the carcasses, and rinse under cold running water to eliminate impurities. Rinse the saucepan and return the carcasses to it. Cover with the water and bring to a boil.

POULTRY FOND BLANC (CON'T)

Add the aromatic garnish, bouillon cube, coarse salt, and peppercorns. Cook 1 ½ to 2 hours, skimming the surface regularly to remove impurities. Then, strain the fond blanc using a chinois, and set aside to cool.

PIGEON JUS

Makes ¾ cup (200 ml)
- ❑ 1¾ lb (800 g) pigeon carcasses
- ❑ 2 shallots
- ❑ 4 tsp (20 ml) grapeseed oil
- ❑ 2 tbsp (30 g) butter
- ❑ 3 cloves garlic
- ❑ ⅓ cup (80 ml) red wine
- ❑ 4 cups or 1 qt (1 L) fond blanc*

Cut the pigeon carcasses into small, even pieces; slice the shallots. Heat the oil in a saucepan over medium heat. Add the carcass pieces and sauté, stirring constantly, for 15 to 20 minutes, until lightly golden. Be careful not to brown the carcasses too much or the jus will taste bitter. Strain using a colander. Discard the all the fat in the saucepan. Place it over high heat; add the butter, garlic, shallots, and carcasses. Sweat* for 5 minutes stirring constantly, to prevent the cooking juices from sticking and burning. Deglaze* with the red wine and reduce* until dry. Moisten with 2 cups (50 cl) of the fond blanc and reduce to a thick, shiny jus*. Coat the carcass pieces with the jus and add the remaining fond blanc. Cook, uncovered, over low heat for 35 to 40 minutes until clear and the jus has thickened slightly.

BASIC RECIPES

PIGEON JUS (CONT'D)

Remove from the heat, and strain using a fine mesh chinois*. Pour the jus and the fat into a bowl—the fat will cover and seal the jus; it will also help bind the jus when used.

SALMIS SAUCE

- ❑ 2 pigeon hearts and livers
- ❑ ⅓ cup (80 ml) pigeon jus*
- ❑ 2 sprigs flat-leaf parsley
- ❑ 2 sprigs chervil
- ❑ 3 chives
- ❑ 1 tbsp (15 ml) sherry vinegar

Finely chop the hearts and livers. Heat the pigeon jus in a sauté pan*, then bind* with the chopped hearts and livers. Chop the herbs and add to the jus. Remove from the heat and infuse* for 10 minutes. Add the vinegar and serve.

SEALING PASTRY

- ❑ 1 ¾ cups or 7 oz (200 g) cake/pastry flour
- ❑ ½ tsp (3 g) salt
- ❑ 5 ½ tbsp (80 g) creamed butter*
- ❑ 1 egg
- ❑ 1 tsp (5 ml) white wine vinegar
- ❑ 1 egg yolk, beaten for glazing

Mix the flour and salt. Then add the butter, egg, and vinegar; mix to combine. Shape the dough into a ball and roll it out into a ribbon, ¹⁄₁₀ inch (2 mm) thick. Moisten the dough with a little water, then "glue" it onto the dish to seal. Brush with beaten egg yolk and place in the oven.

TAPENADE

- ❏ 2 anchovy fillets, in brine
- ❏ 1 clove pink garlic, germ removed
- ❏ 9 oz (250 g) Taggiasca olives, pitted
- ❏ ⅔ cup (150 ml) extra virgin olive oil
- ❏ 4 tsp (20 ml) sherry vinegar
- ❏ Freshly ground black pepper
- ❏ marjoram leaves

Soak the anchovies for 5 minutes in cold water to remove the salt. Put the anchovies and a clove of garlic, germ removed, into a mortar. Pound with the pestle, gradually adding the olives, to obtain a paste. Add the olive oil, gradually pounding until thick. Add the vinegar, pepper, and marjoram leaves.

VEGETABLE BOUILLON

- ❏ 1 lb 2 oz (500 g) vegetable trimmings (see p. 28)
- ❏ 3 ½ tbsp (50 ml) extra virgin olive oil
- ❏ 2 ½ tsp (10 g) coarse salt
- ❏ White peppercorns
- ❏ 1 stalk thyme
- ❏ 1 stalk basil

Roughly chop the vegetable trimmings. Heat the olive oil in a saucepan, add the trimmings loosen and sweat*. Add 2 quarts (2 L) of water and simmer for 30 minutes. Season with coarse salt, white peppercorns, and the herbs. Strain the bouillon twice: first to remove the trimmings, then through a fine-mesh chinois* to clarify.

ALAIN DUCASSE'S ADDRESS BOOK

WWW.ALAIN-DUCASSE.COM

RESTAURANT LE MEURICE ALAIN DUCASSE - HÔTEL LE MEURICE, PARIS

PARIS

**RESTAURANT LE MEURICE
ALAIN DUCASSE
HÔTEL LE MEURICE**
228, RUE DE RIVOLI
75001 PARIS
TÉL. +33 (0)1 44 58 10 55

**ALAIN DUCASSE
AU PLAZA ATHÉNÉE**
25, AVENUE MONTAIGNE
75008 PARIS
TÉL. +33 (0)1 53 67 65 00

MONACO

**LE LOUIS XV ALAIN DUCASSE
HÔTEL DE PARIS**
PLACE DU CASINO
98000 MONACO
TÉL. +377 98 06 88 64

LONDRES

**ALAIN DUCASSE
AT THE DORCHESTER
THE DORCHESTER**
PARK LANE
LONDON W1K 1QA
TEL. +44 (0)20 7629 8866

ALAIN DUCASSE AU PLAZA ATHÉNÉE, PARIS

LE LOUIS XV - ALAIN DUCASSE, MONACO

ALAIN DUCASSE AT THE DORCHESTER, LONDRES

LE JULES VERNE, PARIS

ÉCOLE DE CUISINE ALAIN DUCASSE, PARIS

PARIS

LE JULES VERNE
TOUR EIFFEL
AVENUE GUSTAVE EIFFEL
75007 PARIS

LE RELAIS PLAZA
HÔTEL PLAZA ATHÉNÉE
21, AVENUE MONTAIGNE
75008 PARIS
TÉL. +33 (0)1 53 67 64 00

LA COUR JARDIN
HÔTEL PLAZA ATHÉNÉE
25, AVENUE MONTAIGNE
75008 PARIS
TÉL. +33 (0)1 53 67 66 02

BENOIT
20, RUE SAINT MARTIN
75004 PARIS
TÉL. +33 (0)1 42 72 25 76

AUX LYONNAIS
32, RUE SAINT MARC
75002 PARIS
TÉL. +33 (0)1 42 96 65 04

RECH
62, AVENUE DES TERNES
75017 PARIS
TÉL. +33 (0)1 45 72 29 47

ALLARD
41, RUE SAINT ANDRÉ
DES ARTS
1, RUE DE L'ÉPERON
75006 PARIS
TÉL. +33 (0)1 43 26 48 23

LE CHOCOLAT ALAIN DUCASSE
MANUFACTURE A PARIS
40, RUE DE LA ROQUETTE
75011 PARIS
TÉL. +33 (0)1 48 05 82 86

LE CORNER
DE LA MANUFACTURE
GALERIES LAFAYETTE
GOURMET - MAISON
REZ-DE-CHAUSSEE
35, BOULEVARD HAUSSMANN
75009 PARIS
TÉL. +33 (0)1 42 65 48 26

LE COMPTOIR DE LA MANUFACTURE
26, RUE SAINT-BENOÎT
75006 PARIS
TÉL. +33 (0)1 45 48 87 89

RECH, PARIS

ÉCOLE DE CUISINE
ALAIN DUCASSE
64, RUE DU RANELAGH
75016 PARIS
TÉL. +33 (0)1 44 90 91 00

ÉCOLE DE CUISINE
ALAIN DUCASSE
LE BHV MARAIS
3E ÉTAGE
52, RUE DE RIVOLI
75004 PARIS

ÉCOLE DE CUISINE
ALAIN DUCASSE
GALERIES LAFAYETTE
GOURMET - MAISON
2E ÉTAGE
35, BOULEVARD HAUSSMANN
75008 PARIS

LE CHOCOLAT ALAIN DUCASSE, PARIS

ALLARD, PARIS

AUX LYONNAIS, PARIS

ALAIN DUCASSE'S ADDRESS BOOK

WWW.ALAIN-DUCASSE.COM

MOUSTIERS SAINTE MARIE

LA BASTIDE DE MOUSTIERS
CHEMIN DE QUINSON
04360 MOUSTIERS
SAINTE MARIE
TÉL. +33 (0)4 92 70 47 47

LA CELLE EN PROVENCE

HOSTELLERIE DE L'ABBAYE DE LA CELLE
10, PLACE DU GÉNÉRAL
DE GAULLE
83170 LA CELLE
EN PROVENCE
TÉL. +33 (0)4 98 05 14 14

SAINT TROPEZ

**RIVEA AT BYBLOS
HÔTEL BYBLOS**
AVENUE MARÉCHAL FOCH
83990 SAINT TROPEZ
TÉL. +33 (0)4 94 56 68 20

MONACO

**LA TRATTORIA
SPORTING
MONTE-CARLO**
AVENUE PRINCESSE
GRACE
98000 MONACO
TÉL. +377 98 06 71 71

**LE GRILL
HÔTEL DE PARIS**
PLACE DU CASINO
98000 MONACO
TÉL. +377 98 06 88 88

CASTIGLIONE DELLA PESCAIA (TOSCANE)

L'ANDANA
TENUTA LA BADIOLA
LOCALITÀ BADIOLA
58043 CASTIGLIONE DELLA
PESCAIA (GR)
TÉL. +39 (0) 564 944 800

DOHA

IDAM
MUSEUM OF ISLAMIC ART
5TH FLOOR, DOHA,
QUATAR
TÉL. +974 4422 4488

L'HOSTELLERIE DE L'ABBAYE DE LA CELLE, LA CELLE EN PROVENCE

L'HOSTELLERIE DE L'ABBAYE DE LA CELLE, LA CELLE EN PROVENCE

L'ANDANA TENUTA LA BADIOLA, CASTIGLIONE DELLA PESCAIA

LA BASTIDE DE MOUSTIERS,
MOUSTIERS SAINTE MARIE

MIX NEVADA, LAS VEGAS

MIX, ST. PETERSBURG

SPOON BY ALAIN DUCASSE, HONG KONG

BEIGE ALAIN DUCASSE, TOKYO

BENOIT, NEW YORK

BEIGE ALAIN DUCASSE, TOKYO

NEW YORK

BENOIT
60 WEST 55TH STREET
NEW YORK, NY 10019
TÉL. +1 (646) 943 7373

LAS VEGAS

RIVÉA
HOTEL DELANO
3950 LAS VEGAS
BOULEVARD,
LAS VEGAS NEVADA 89119
TÉL. +1 (702) 632 95 00

HONG KONG

SPOON
BY ALAIN DUCASSE
INTERCONTINENTAL
HONG-KONG,
18 SALISBURY ROAD,
KOWLOON, HONG KONG
TÉL. +852 23 13 22 56

TOKYO

BEIGE ALAIN DUCASSE
GINZA CHANEL BUILDING
L0F
3-5-3 GINZA, CHUO-KU,
104-0061 TOKYO
TÉL. + 81 (3) 5159 5500

BENOIT
LA PORTE AOYAMA 10F,
5-51-8 JINGUMAE
SHIBUYA-KU,
150-0001 TOKYO
TÉL. + 81 (3) 6419 4181

SAINT PETERSBURG

MIX IN ST. PETERSBURG
HOTEL W
ST. PETERSBURG
VOZNESENSKY PROSPEKT,
6, ST. PETERSBURG,
190000
TEL. +7 (812) 610 61 66

PRODUCT INDEX

BENOIT WITZ

A chef with more than twenty years of experience, Benoit Witz joined Alain Ducasse's the Louis XV restaurant in Monaco in 1987. In 1996, he became chef at La Bastide de Moustiers, then at the Hostellerie de l'Abbaye de La Celle. At the same time, he teaches cooking and has written several recipe books.

CHRISTIAN JULLIARD

In 1992, Christian Julliard joined Alain Ducasse as an "itinerant chef." Trained at the Louis XV, he has been involved in a number of restaurant openings. He has served as Corporate Chef of the Alain Ducasse Group since 2006. His savoir faire and culinary philosophy are based on simplicity and respect for produce.

Distributed in North America by Stewart, Tabori & Chang, an imprint of ABRAMS.

Abrams books are available at special discounts when purchased in quantity for premiums and promotions as well as fundraising or educational use. Special editions can also be created to specification. For details, contact specialsales@abramsbooks.com or the address below.

THE ART OF BOOKS SINCE 1949

115 West 18th Street
New York, NY 10011
www.abramsbooks.com

COLLECTION DIRECTOR
Emmanuel Jirou-Najou

EDITORIAL MANAGER
Alice Gouget

PUBLISHING MANAGER
Églantine Lefébure

PHOTOGRAPHY
Valérie Guedes and Pierre Monetta (cover and pages 2/5)

ARTISTIC DIRECTOR
Pierre Tachon

GRAPHIC DESIGN
Soins graphiques
Thanks to Sophie

RECIPE CREATION
Christian Julliard and Benoit Witz
A huge thank-you to Franck Geuffroy

DRINK PAIRING
Gérard Margeon and Guillem Kerambrun

PHOTOENGRAVING
Nord Compo

PROOFREADER
Karine Elsener

MARKETING AND COMMUNICATION MANAGER
Camille Gonnet
camille.gonnet@alain-ducasse.com

Printed in China
ISBN : 978-2-84123-728-9
Legal deposit : 4th semester 2014

© ALAIN DUCASSE Édition 2014
84 avenue Victor Cresson
92441 Issy-Les-Moulineaux Cedex
www.alain-ducasse.com/fr/les-livres

COOK
WITH YOUR
FAVORITE
CHEFS

PIERRE
HERMÉ
ALAIN DUCASSE
PUBLISHING

ERIC
RIPERT
ALAIN DUCASSE
PUBLISHING

DANIEL
BOULUD
ALAIN DUCASSE
PUBLISHING

my BEST

ILLUSTRATED **COOKING COURSES** FROM **FINEST CHEFS** TO HELP YOU PRODUCE THEIR **TOP 10 RECIPES** WITH PERFECT RESULTS EVERY TIME!

ALAIN DUCASSE

www.alain-ducasse.com